Quick Russian

Diethard Lübke

TEACH YOURSELF BOOKS
Hodder and Stoughton

British Library Cataloguing in Publication Data

Lubke, Diethard
  Teach yourself quick and easy Russian.
  I. Title
  491.78

  ISBN 0-340-55063-5

First published 1990 by Langenscheidt Publishers

© 1991 Hodder and Stoughton Ltd

Typeset by Transet Typesetters, Coventry, England
Printed in Great Britain for the educational publishing division of Hodder and
Stoughton Ltd, Mill Road, Dunton Green, Sevenoaks, Kent by Clays Ltd, St.
Ives plc, Bungay, Suffolk.

Contents

Introduction

This course of self study aims to help you understand and speak simple Russian, the sort of Russian you will need on a visit to the USSR. It cannot promise that at the end you will be speaking perfectly, but by enabling you to learn the most important words and expressions a visitor needs, it will undoubtedly help to improve your experience of the Soviet Union and get more out of your time abroad.

The course does not require a great deal of study, but it does offer more than a phrasebook and you will find that if you are prepared to spend a certain amount of time, even at odd hours of the day, in going through each unit in turn and testing your knowledge carefully, you will begin to acquire a basic knowledge of the language.

About six weeks before you trip, start looking at the Russian alphabet on pages 6–7, then work your way through the examples on pages 8–10. Try to work out how each word is pronounced, looking back at the alphabet if you get stuck, and check in the Answers to see if you have guessed the meaning correctly. When you feel you have mastered this sufficiently, move on to the 20 units.

Each unit deals with a particular aspect of a visit to the USSR, and contains groups of words and phrases with their approximate pronunciation in English phonetics, followed by English translations. Look at them carefully and read them aloud, referring back to the section on the Russian alphabet if necessary. If you have the cassette, look at the book as you listen, and practise repeating each word or phrase. The exercises that follow are to reinforce what you have learned and to test that you have grasped the basic language needed to cope with the situations most likely to occur. For example, as well as ordering food, making purchases, dealing with public transport and so on in simple Russian, you are asked to work out the information given on a ticket and a shop notice, and to decipher simple street and road signs.

At the end of each unit is a short information section in English which you will find useful on your visit. Take the book with you when you go to the USSR, so that you can practise the words and phrases you have learnt. Don't be afraid to use them – you are bound to make mistakes, but the most important thing is that you will have made yourself understood.

The Russian Alphabet

It is not very hard to speak Russian – the main difficulty for beginners is the Russian script. However, if you persevere, you'll find that you soon get used to the Russian alphabet.

You already know several Russian letters. The following are the same as or very similar to English:

А	а	=	*a*
Е	е	=	*e*
К	к	=	*k*
М	м	=	*m*
О	о	=	*o*
Т	т	=	*t*

Some letters look like English, but are pronounced differently:

В	в	=	*v*
Н	н	=	*n*
Р	р	=	*r*
С	с	=	*s*
У	у	=	*u (oo)*
Х	х	=	*ch* (as in *loch*)

The following Russian letters do not appear in the English alphabet:

Б	б	=	*b*
Г	г	=	*g*
Д	д	=	*d*
Ё	ё	=	*yo*
Ж	ж	=	*su* (as in *leisure*)
З	з	=	*z*
И	и	=	*ee*
Й	й	=	*i*
Л	л	=	*l*
П	п	=	*p*
Ф	ф	=	*f*
Ц	ц	=	*ts*
Ч	ч	=	*ch*
Ш	ш	=	*sh*
Щ	щ	=	*shch*
Ъ	ъ	=	hard sign (not pronounced)

The Russian Alphabet

Ы	ы	=	*iy*
Ь	ь	=	soft sign (not pronounced)
Э	э	=	*e*
Ю	ю	=	*yoo*
Я	я	=	*ya*

Some points to note:

Russian words are strongly stressed, and the syllable which carries the stress is marked with an accent (´) in this book. Vowels which are unstressed are weaker than those that carry the stress: for example, unstressed **o** is pronounced more like *a*, unstressed **e** and **я** like *i*.

The phonetic pronunciation used here is intended to follow English sounds as far as possible. However, note that **ye** at the end of a word is pronounced as in *yet;* **kh** is the sound *ch* in *loch;* **zh** is the sound *su* in *leisure.*

Here is the complete Russian in alphabet in the order in which it appears:

А	Б	В	Г	Д	Е	Ё	Ж	З	И	Й
К	Л	М	Н	О	П	Р	С	Т	У	Ф
Х	Ц	Ч	Ш	Щ	Ъ	Ы	Ь	Э	Ю	Я

Practise the Russian Alphabet

Compare the following:

ПРАВДА
PRAVDA

ЛЕНИН
LENIN

АЭРОФЛОТ
AEROFLOT

МОСКВА
MOSKVA (MOSCOW)

МЕТРО
METRO

ПЕРЕСТРОЙКА
PERESTROIKA

СПУТНИК
SPUTNIK

ВОДКА
VODKA

АННА
ANNA

КРЕМЛЬ
KREML (KREMLIN)

ГЛАСНОСТЬ
GLASNOST

Russian contains a lot of foreign words, many of which you know already.
What do the following words mean?

турист

....

банк

....

бюро

....

чек

....

касса

....

....

фильм

....

телефон

....

театр

....

опера

....

балет

....

концерт

....

университет ....

Practise the Russian Alphabet

профессор   экономист   студент

....

институт   диплом

....

микроскоп

....

каталог   лексикон

....

литература

....

журнал   Толстой   Анна Каренина

....

актриса   радио

....

(a)	**да** da	*yes*
	нет nyet	*no*
	конечно kanyéshna	*of course*
	хорошо kharashó	*good, OK*
(b)	**доброе утро** dóbroye óotra	*good morning*
	здравствуйте zdrástvooeetye	*hello/good day* (used at any time of day)
	до свидания da sveedáneeya	*goodbye*

Здравствуй, Пётр Zdrástvooee, Pyotr	*Hello, Peter*
Здравствуйте, Пётр и Таня Zdrástvooeetye, Pyotr ee Tánya	*Hello, Peter and Tanya*
Как дела? Kak dyelá?	*How are you?*
Хорошо Kharashó	*Fine*

(c)	**пожалуйста** pazhálasta	*please*
	спасибо spaséeba	*thank you*

1 General Expressions

простите prastéetye	*excuse me*
ничего neechevó	*that's OK/don't mention it*

Большое спасибо Balshóye spaséeba	*Thank you very much*

(*d*)

товарищ* taváreeshch	*comrade*
господин* gaspadéen	*Mr*
госпожа* gaspazhá	*Mrs*

*See note on page 14

(*e*)

Это ... Éta ...	*This/That is ...*
этот, эта, это état, éta, éta	*this* (masc.) *this* (fem.), *this* (neuter)
Вот ... Vot ...	*Here is ...*

Это дом Éta dom	*This is a house*
этот дом état dom	*this house*

(*f*)

я ya	*I*
мой, моя, моё moy, mayá, mayó	*my* (m.), *my* (f.), *my* (n.)
мои mayée	*my* (plural)
вы viy	*you*
ваш, ваша, ваше vash, vásha, váshe	*your* (m.), *your* (f.), *your* (n.)
ваши váshee	*your* (pl.)

мой чемодан moy chimadán	*my suitcase*
Ваш паспорт, пожалуйста Vash páspart, pazhálasta	*Your passport, please*
Вот мой паспорт Vot moy passpart	*Here is my passport*

General Expressions 1

1. You have just met Пётр. How do you say hello to him?

   ....

2. He asks you how you are. What does he say?

   ....

3. Tell him that you're fine.

   ....

4. Now it's time to say goodbye. What do you say in Russian?

   ....

5. You arrive at the hotel and say hello to the 'administrator' (manager) in the reception area:

   ....

6. The manager wants to see your passport. What does he ask you?

   ....

7. You hand him your passport. What do you say?

   ....

8. The manager thanks you – what does he say?

   ....

9. The hotel manager wants to know if this suitcase belongs to you.

   (a) If it's yours, what do you tell him?

   ....

   (b) If it isn't yours, what do you say?

   ....

1 General Expressions

10. Someone jostles you in the metro. How does he apologise?

....

11. Tell him 'That's OK'.

....

- There is no article (*the, a*) in Russian:

  дом = *house/the house/a house*
- '*Is*' and '*are*' are generally omitted:

  Это дом = *This/that (is) (a) house*

  Я Пётр = *I (am) Peter*
- Russian has three genders, i.e. all nouns are either masculine (words ending in a consonant), feminine (those ending in **–a** or **–я**) and neuter (those ending in **–o** or **–e**).
- There are six grammatical 'cases': nominative, accusative, genitive, dative, instrumental and locative (also known as prepositional). This means that in Russian, many words change their endings depending on where they come in a sentence, after certain prepositions, and so on. However, the core of the word generally stays the same.
- Russian has no real equivalent to *Mr, Mrs* or *Miss,* and this can create difficulties. It is not appropriate for Western tourists to use the word **товарищ** (*comrade*), and the antiquated terms **господин** and **госпожа** (*Mr, Mrs*) sound stiff and rather ridiculous. Russians have three names – first name, patronymic (taken from the father's name), and surname. If you are introduced to someone by their first name and patronymic, you should address them by these two names. This is the polite form of address in the Soviet Union.

Добро пожаловать в Советский Союз!
Welcome to the Soviet Union!

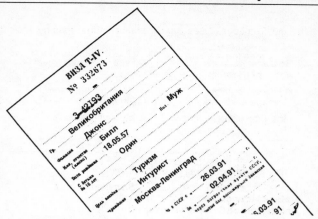

(a)
поездка payézdka	*journey*
таможня tamózhnya	*customs*
багаж bagázh	*luggage*
чемодан chimadán	*suitcase*
сумка sóomka	*handbag*

Откройте, пожалуйста, чемодан Atkróitye, pazhálasta, chimadán	*Open your suitcase, please*
таможенная декларация tamózhinnaya diklarátseeya	*customs declaration*
цель поездки tsyel payézdkee	*purpose of journey*

туризм tooréezm	*tourism*

(b)
паспорт páspart	*passport*
виза véeza	*visa*
фамилия faméeleeya	*surname*
имя éemya	*first name*
дата рождения dáta razhdýeneeya	*date of birth*
пол pol	*sex*
адрес ádris	*address*
подпись pódpees	*signature*

2 Arrival and Departure

паспортный контроль páspartniy kantról	*passport control*
Вот мой паспорт Vot moy páspart	*Here is my passport*
Ваша фамилия? Vásha faméeleeya?	*What is your name (surname)?*
Моя фамилия – Jones Mayá faméeleeya Jones	*My name is Jones*

(c)
гражданство grázhdanstva	*nationality*
Союз Советских Социалистических Республик (СССР) Sayóoz Savýetskeekh Satsiyalistéech-iskeekh Rispoobléek (Es-Es-Es-Er)	*Soviet Union*
Великобритания Vileekabreetáneeya	*Great Britain*
Англия Ángleeya	*England*
из Англии eez Ánglee'ee	*from England*
Шотландия Shatlándeeya	*Scotland*
Уэльс Ooéls	*Wales*
Америка Amýereeka	*America*
Канада Kanáda	*Canada*
Австралия Afstráleeya	*Australia*
Новая Зеландия Nóvaya Zilándeeya	*New Zealand*
англичанин angleecháneen	*Englishman*
англичанка angleechánka	*Englishwoman*
английский angléeskee	*English (adjective)*
посольство pasólstva	*embassy*
консульство kónsoolstva	*consulate*

Я англичанин/англичанка Ya angleecháneen/ angleechánka	*I am English (m., f.)*
Вы говорите по-английски? Viy gavaréetye pa-angléeskee?	*Do you speak English?*
Я не понимаю Ya ni paneemáyoo	*I don't understand*

Translate these two signs, which you will come across in the Soviet Union.

ПАСПОРТНЫЙ КОНТРОЛЬ   ТАМОЖНЯ

1. ....   2. ....

What are these items of luggage called in Russian?

3. ....   4. ....

5. The customs officer asks whether you are English. If you are, what do you say?

   ....

6. Now tell him where you come from.

   ....

7. He asks your name – what does he say?

   ....

8. You are Mrs Jones. Tell the customs officer.

   ....

9. What do you say if you don't understand something in Russian?

   ....

2 Arrival and Departure

10. What are these three countries called in Russian:

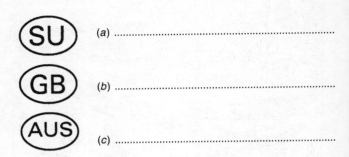

(a) ....

(b) ....

(c) ....

- On entering the Soviet Union, visitors must fill in a customs declaration. You are required to state the amount of money you are carrying (it is illegal to bring roubles into the country) as well as any valuables such as cameras and jewellery. The customs officer will sign the declaration and return it to you.

- You must produce the customs declaration whenever you change money so that the transaction can be entered.

- If you buy anything expensive in a Beriozka shop (see Unit 9 (c)) you should keep the receipt for presentation at customs on your departure.

- When leaving the country, you will have to fill in another customs declaration. You will need to declare the same valuables as on arrival, and the balance of your money. Both declarations should be handed in.

(a) **автомобиль** aftamabéel ⎫
    машина mashéena   ⎬   *car*
    права pravá   *driving licence*
    грузовик groozavéek   *lorry*
    шина shéena   *tyre*

(b) **дорога** daróga   *road*
    проспект praspýekt   *long straight road, avenue*
    шоссе shassáy   *main road, chaussee*
    автомагистраль aftamageestrál *motorway*

> **Невский проспект**   *Nevsky Prospekt* (main street
> Nýefskee praspýekt   in Leningrad)

(c) **заправочная станция**   *petrol station*
    zaprávachnaya stántseeya
    бензин binzéen   *petrol*
    масло másla   *oil*

3 Driving a Car

| пункт технического обслуживания
poonkt tikhnéechiskava apslóozheevaneeya | repairs garage |

| **Где заправочная станция?**
Gdye zaprávachnaya stántseeya? | *Where's the petrol station?* |
| **Тридцать литров бензина**
Tréedsat léetraf binzéena | *30 litres of petrol* |

(d)   **(авто) стоянка**
(afta) stayánka
стоп! stop!   car park

stop!

| **Стоянка запрещена!**
Stayánka zaprishchiná! | *No parking!* |
| **Одностороннее движение**
Adnastarónyee dveezhéneeye | *One-way street* |

What are these in Russian?

1. ....   2. ....

What do these road signs mean in Russian?

3. .... 4. .... 5. ....

6. Where does the scene in this picture take place?

....

3 Driving a Car

- It is possible to take your own car to the Soviet Union or to hire a car. However, Western tourists should keep to appointed routes and the entire journey must be agreed in advance with Intourist.

- The speed limit is 60 kph (37 mph) in built-up areas, 90 kph (56 mph) elsewhere. Cars tend to drive rather fast in towns, and drivers do not always pay much attention to pedestrians!

- At night, cars drive on side-lights in built-up areas.

- There are few petrol stations compared to Western countries – look out for the road signs.

- When parking for any length of time, it is usual to remove wing mirrors and windscreen wipers and keep them locked inside your car.

- There is little traffic on long-distance routes. The busiest roads are Brest–Minsk–Moscow and Leningrad–Moscow.

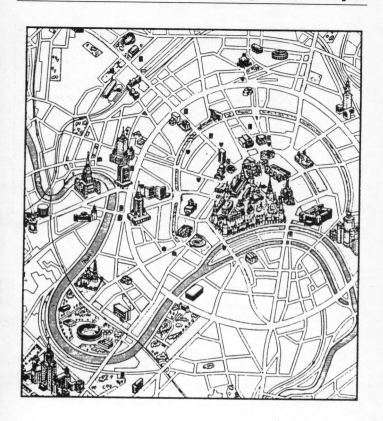

(a) **карта** kárta — *map*

карта города kárta górada — *town plan*

дорожная карта darózhnaya kárta — *road map*

Карта Москвы, пожалуйста
Kárta Maskvíy, pazhálasta — *A map of Moscow, please*

4 Finding Your Way

(b)   **город** górat   *town*
     столица staléetsa   *capital*
     дом dom   *house*

> **центр города**   *town centre*
> tsentr górada

(c)   **улица (ул.)** óoleetsa   *street*
     проспект praspýekt   *main street, avenue*
     бульвар boolvár   *boulevard*
     переулок piríoolak   *alley*
     площадь plóshchat   *square*
     мост most   *bridge*
     переход pirikhót   *underpass* (for pedestrians)

> **Красная площадь**   *Red Square*
> Krásnaya plóshchat
>
> **проспект Маркса**   *Marx Prospekt*
> praspýekt Márksa

(d)   **Где ...?** Gdye ...?   *Where (is) ...?*
     тут toot   *here*
     там tam   *there*
     налево nalyéva   *left, to the left*
     направо napráva   *right, to the right*
     прямо pryáma   *straight on*
     север syévir   *north*
     юг yook   *south*
     восток vastók   *east*
     запад zápat   *west*

> **Где улица Горького?**   *Where's Gorky Street?*
> Gdye óoleetsa Górkava?
>
> **Где вокзал?** Gdye vakzál?   *Where's the station?*

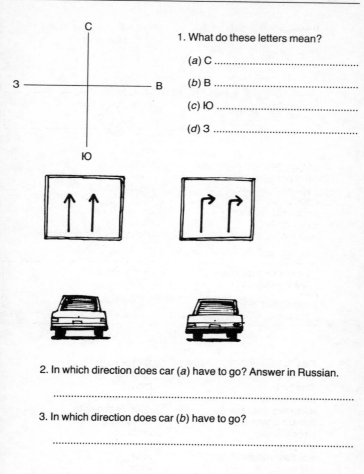

1. What do these letters mean?

(a) C ....

(b) B ....

(c) Ю ....

(d) З ....

2. In which direction does car (a) have to go? Answer in Russian.

....

3. In which direction does car (b) have to go?

....

4. You want to get to the other side of the street. What does this sign indicate?

....

At the Underground exit, you see this sign: Exit to the street.

5. Which way do you go if you want to get to Red Square?

....

6. Which way do you go if you want to get to Marx Prospekt?

You come out onto the street and see this sign:

ПРОСПЕКТ
МАРКСА

7. Are you really in Marx Prospekt? (Answer using **да** or **нет.**)

- It is advisable to buy street and road maps at home and bring them with you on your journey.
- In large towns you are expected to cross main roads using one of the many underpasses (**переход**).

(a)
вокзал vakzál		*station*
путь poot		*track, platform*
поезд póyizd		*train*
спальный вагон spálniy vagón		*sleeping car*
вагон-ресторан vagón-ristarán		*dining car*

Белорусский вокзал Bilaróoskee vakzál	*White Russian Station*
Ленинградский вокзал Liningrátskee vakzál	*Leningrad station*
Но. поезда Nómir póyizda	*train number*

(b)
аэропорт aerapórt	*airport*
вылет víylit	*flight (departure)*
самолёт samalýot	*aeroplane*
АЭРОФЛОТ aeraflót	*AEROFLOT (state airline)*

Аэропорт Шереметьево 2 Aerapórt Shirimýetiva dva	*Sheremetevo 2 Airport (international flights)*
Но. рейса nómir ryéisa	*flight number*
Застегнуть ремни! Zastignóot ryémnee!	*Fasten your seatbelts!*

(c)
пароход parakhót	*steamer*
каюта kayóota	*cabin*
ракета rakyéta	*hydrofoil*

5 Public Transport

(d)

автобус aftóboos	bus	
троллейбус trallyéiboos	trolleybus	
трамвай tramvái	tram	
остановка astanófka	stop (bus etc)	
метро mitró	Metro, (underground)	
станция stántseeya	station (metro)	
переход pirikhót	connections (when changing trains)	
такси taksée	taxi	
стоянка такси stayánka taksée	taxi rank	

"Следующая станция: Комсомольская!" 'Slyéduyooshchaya stánteseeya: Kamsamólskaya'	'Next station: Komsomolskaya!'
К вокзалу, пожалуйста! K vakzáloo, pazhálasta!	To the station, please!
Остановитесь, пожалуйста! Astanavéetyes, pazhálasta!	Stop, please!

(e)

информация eenfarmátseeya	information
справки spráfkee	enquiries
расписание raspeesáneeye	timetable
окно aknó	window
касса kássa	cashdesk, ticket office
билет beelyét	ticket
вход fkhot	entrance
выход víykhat	exit
пассажир passazhéer	passenger

Ваши билеты, пожалуйста! Váshee beelyétiy, pazhálasta!	Tickets please!
выход в город víykhat f_górat	exit to the town
запасной выход zapasnóy víykhat	emergency exit

You are at the railway station in Moscow and see this sign.

1. Which platform is the train at?

....

2. Where is the train going to?

....

3. You want to leave the station, and you see this sign. Can you say what it means in English?

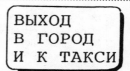

....

Look at this map of the Underground in central Moscow and see if you can find these stations: Komsomolskaya, Prospekt Mira, Belorusskaya, Prospekt Marksa and Kievskaya.

4. Now you are at Prospekt Mira and hear the loudspeaker announcing the name of the next station. Which one is it?

....

5. You are at Belorusskaya going towards the city centre. What is the next station?

....

5 Public Transport

6. What announcement do you hear at Kievskaya?

....

[Ticket stamp:]
Ленинградский
ТРОЛЛЕЙБУС
Сер. О-048
482828
КОНТРОЛЬНЫЙ
БИЛЕТ
№ 19 с 28 до 82

Look at this ticket.

7. For what form of transport is it valid?

....

8. In which town? ....

- To travel by Underground, you need a 5-kopeck piece. At the entrance to every station there are automatic change machines which take 10-, 15- and 20-kopeck coins. You insert the 5-kopeck piece into a slot in the barrier and a green light indicates that you can pass. You do not get a ticket.

- All metro signs are written in Cyrillic script only. There are maps of the Underground system on the wall at station entrances and train destinations are shown on the platform on white illuminated boards. Before you board the train, try to remember how many stops there are until your station – and listen out for the announcement.

- Underground trains only stop for a few moments, so make haste when boarding a train!

- In most Soviet cities, tickets for buses, trams, etc. can be bought from kiosks (usually in books of ten) as well as on the bus itself.

- Taxis can be recognised by a sign on the roof or a **T** on the door. An illuminated green light behind the windscreen shows that the taxi is free.

- In addition, private cars will often stop if you put your arm out, and will take you to your destination for a small fee in the same way as taxis.

(a) **ИНТУРИСТ** eentooréest   *INTOURIST*
гость gost   *guest*
гостиница gastéeneetsa   *hotel*
кемпинг kémpeeng   *campsite*
администратор   *manager, official in charge*
admeeneestrátar

Пожалуйста, к гостинице "Космос"! Pazhálasta, k gastéeneetsi 'Kosmos'!	(to taxi driver) *Hotel Kosmos, please!*

6 Accommodation

(b)

комната kómnata	room
номер nómir	hotel room, number
постель pastýel	bed
ванная vánnaya	bathroom
ванна vánna	bath
душ doosh	shower
вода vadá	water
ключ klyooch	key
лифт leeft	lift
этаж etázh	floor, storey
1-ый этаж pyérviy etázh*	ground floor

*Literally 'first floor' in Russian

дежурная по этажу dizhóornaya pạ etazhóo	floor attendant (usually female)
Пожалуйста, ключ от **номера сто двадцать** Pazhálasta, klyooch at nómira sto dvátsat	The key to room 120, please
одноместный номер adnamyéstniy nómir	single room
двухместный номер dvookhmyéstniy nómir	double room

(c)

стоимость номера stóymast ńomira	price of the room
Сколько стоит номер? Skólka stóyit nómir?	How much is the room?
квитанция kveetántseeya	receipt

(d)

туалеты twalyétiy	toilets
Ж (женский) (zhénskee)	Ladies'
М (мужской) (moozhskóy)	Gentlemen's

Где туалеты? Gdye twalyétiy?	Where are the toilets?
занято zányata	engaged
свободно svabódna	vacant

What are these in Russian?

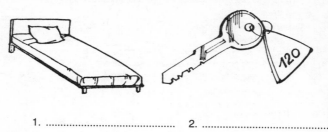

1. .... 2. ....

3. You want the key to room number 120. What do you say to the lady in charge of your corridor?

....

4. You are in the lift and want to go to the ground floor. Which button do you press?

....

What amenities do these road signs indicate? Give your answer in Russian.

5. .... 6. ....

6 Accommodation

7. You want to know where the toilet is. How do you ask?

....?

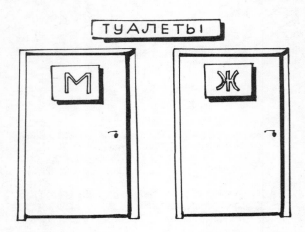

8. Is the Ladies' the door on the right-hand side? Answer using **да** or **нет**.

....

– Many hotels in the Soviet Union still use the system of corridor attendants who keep an eye on the rooms on each floor. In these hotels you don't get your key from reception, as elsewhere; instead, you are given a card with your room number on it (**визиточка** veezéetachka) and you give this to the corridor lady in exchange for your key. When you go out, you should hand over your key and retrieve your hotel card – you will not be able to get back into the hotel without showing it at the door.

– The voltage in Soviet hotels is generally 220v. It is advisable to take an adaptor with you.

НА АВТОМАТИЧЕСКОЙ СВЯЗИ БОЛЕЕ 300 ГОРОДОВ

Сняв телефонную трубку, набрав цифру 8, вы услышите сигнал о возможности выхода на автоматическую междугородную связь. Далее следует набрать цифры кода нужного вам города.

Город	Код	Город	Код
АЛМА-АТА *	327	БУХАРА	365
АНДИЖАН *	374	ВИЛЬНЮС	012
АРХАНГЕЛЬСК	818	ВИТЕБСК *	021
АСТРАХАНЬ	851	ВЛАДИМИР	092
Астраханской обл.		(с 14 до 9 часов;	
Икряное	85114	в выходн. и празд.—	
Красный Яр	85116	круглосуточно)	
АШХАБАД	363	ВОЛГОГРАД *	844
БАКУ	892	Волгоградской обл.	
БАРНАУЛ *	385	Волжский	84459
Алтайского края		Камышин	84457
Алейск	38553	Михайловка	84463
Бийск	38538	Урюпинск	84442
Благовещенка	38564	ВОЛОГДА *	817
Волчиха	38565	ВОРОНЕЖ	073
Камень-на-Оби	38514	ВОРОШИЛОВГРАД *	
Кулунда	38566		064
Мамонтово	38513	Ворошиловградской обл.	
Рубцовск	38557	Антрацит	06431
Славгород	38558	Беловодск	06466
Смоленское	38536	Брянка	06443
Тальменка	38591	Красный Луч	06432
Троицкое	38534	Краснодон	06435
Целинное	38596	Коммунарск	06442
БЕЛГОРОД *	072	Кременная	06454
Белгородской обл.		Кировск	06446
Алексеевка	07234	Лисичанск	06451
Борисовка	07246	Марковка	06464
Валуйки	07236	Меловое	06465
Вейделевка	07237	Первомайск	06455
Волоконовка	07235	Перевальск	06441
Губкин	07241	Рубежное	06453
Ивня	07243	Ровеньки	06433
Короча	07231	Свердловск	06434
Красногвардей-	07247	Северодонецк	06452
ское		Старобельск	06461

Город	Код	Город	Код
Кулебаки	83176	Кондрово	08434
Павлово	83171	Малоярославец	084031
Семёнов	83162	Обнинск	08139
ГРОДНО *	015	КАРАГАНДА	321
ГРОЗНЫЙ	871	КЕМЕРОВО *	384
ГУЛИСТАН *	367	Кемеровской обл.	
ДЖИЗАК	372	Прокопьевск	38445
ДНЕПРОПЕТРОВСК		КИШИНЕВ	042
	056	КИЕВ *	044
ДОНЕЦК *	062	КИРОВ	833
Донецкой обл.		КИРОВОГРАД	052
Артёмовск	06274	КОСТРОМА *	094
Волноваха	06214	КРАСНОДАР	861
Горловка	06242	КРАСНОЯРСК *	391
Дружковка	06267	КУЙБЫШЕВ *	846
Енакиево	06252	КУРГАН	352
Жданов	06292	КУРСК	071
Краматорск	06264	КУСТАНАЙ *	314
Красноармейск	06239	ЛЕНИНГРАД	812
Константиновка	06272	ЛИПЕЦК	074
Макеевка	06232	ЛУЦК	033
Славянск	06262	ЛЬВОВ *	032
Снежное	06256	Львовской обл.	
Харцызск	06257	Борислав	032483

Наименование	Ёмкость	Цена за бут.	Цена за 100 гр.
I. ВОДКА			
Водка «Экстра» русская	0,5	9-70	1-94
Водка «Русская»	0,5	9-40	1-88
Водка «Особая» столичная	0,5	11-40	2-28
Водка «Охотничья»	0,5	13-20	2-64
Старка	0,7	19-80	
юбилейная	0,75	19-80	2-74
адмиралтейская	0,75	17-10	2-28
зубровка	0,75	17-10	2-28

7 Numbers, Weights and Measures

(a)

1	один, одна*	adéen, adná		19	девятнадцать	divitnatsat
	одно*	adnó		20	двадцать	dvátsat
2	два	dva		21	двадцать один	dvátsat adéen
3	три	tree		22	двадцать два	dvátsat dva
4	четыре	chitíyre		30	тридцать	tréedsat
5	пять	pyat		40	сорок	sórak
6	шесть	shest		50	пятьдесят	pitdisyát
7	семь	syem		60	шестьдесят	shisdisyát
8	восемь	vósim		70	семьдесят	syémdisyat
9	девять	dyévit		80	восемьдесят	vósimdisyat
10	десять	dyésit		90	девяносто	divinósta
11	одиннадцать	adéenatsat		100	сто	sto
12	двенадцать	dvinátsat		110	сто десять	sto dyésit
13	тринадцать	treenátsat		200	двести	dvýestee
14	четырнадцать	chitíyrnatsat		1000	тысяча	tíysicha
15	пятнадцать	pitnátsat		2000	две тысячи	dvye tíysichee
16	шестнадцать	shisnátsat		10 000	десять тысяч	dyésit tíysich
17	семнадцать	simnátsat		1 000 000	миллион	meelión
18	восемнадцать	vosimnátsat				

(b)

грамм gram		*gram*
кило keeló		*kilo*
полкило palkeeló		*half a kilo*
сколько skólka		*how much, how many*
много mnóga		*a lot*
немного nimnóga		*a little*

пятьдесят грамм водки pitdisyát gram vótkee	*50 grams of vodka*
сто грамм водки sto gram vótkee	*100 grams of vodka*

In which rooms are these hotel guests staying?

1. Mr Ivanov: .... 2. Mr Kuznetsov: ....

*masc., fem., neuter

3. Mr Richards ....   4. Mrs Robinson ....

From which platforms do the following trains depart?

5. The train to Leningrad ....

6. The train to Tallin ....

7. The train to Murmansk ....

8. Give the name of this Soviet aeroplane **(ИЛ 62)** in Russian?

....

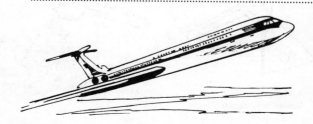

9. How many people are there in this group of tourists?

....

10. How many ladies are there? ....

11. How many men are there? ....

You are in a restaurant. See if you can order some vodka:

12. Order 50 grams of vodka: ....

13. Order 100 grams of vodka: ....

(a) **часы** chasíy — *watch, clock*
час chas — *hour*
минута meenóota — *minute*

> – When using Russian numbers, the following rules should be observed:
>
> – After number 1, the noun stays in its basic, unaltered form.
>
> – After numbers 2 to 4, it goes into the genitive singular.
>
> – After numbers from 5 onwards, the noun goes into the genitive plural. To see how it works, look at the different endings after **минута** and **час**:
>
> | 1 **минута** | adná meenóota | 1 **час** | adéen chas |
> |---|---|---|---|
> | 2 **минуты** | dvye meenóotiy | 2 **часа** | dva chasá |
> | 3 **минуты** | tree meenóotiy | 3 **часа** | tree chasá |
> | 4 **минуты** | chitíyre meenóotiy | 4 **часа** | chitíyre chasá |
> | 5 **минут** | pyat meenóot | 5 **часов** | pyat chasóf |
> | 6 **минут** | shest meenóot | 6 **часов** | shest chasóf |
> | etc. | | | |

8 Time and Dates

Который час? Katóriy chas? — *What time is it?*
Час Chas — *(It's) one o'clock*
Восемь часов Vósyem chasóf — *(It's) eight o'clock*
Когда? Kagdá? — *When?*
В два часа F dva chasá — *At two o'clock*
В шесть часов десять минут — *At twenty past six*
F shest chasóf dyésit meenóot

(*b*)
день dyen — *day*
утро óotra — *morning*
полдень póldin — *midday*
вечер vyéchir — *evening*
ночь noch — *night*
сегодня sivódnya — *today*
вчера fchirá — *yesterday*
завтра záftra — *tomorrow*

(*c*)
время vrémya — *time*
неделя nidyélya — *week*
понедельник panidyélneek — *Monday*
вторник ftórneek — *Tuesday*
среда sridá — *Wednesday*
четверг chitvyérk — *Thursday*
пятница pyátneetsa — *Friday*
суббота soobóta — *Saturday*
воскресенье vaskrisyénye — *Sunday*
месяц myésyits — *month*
год got — *year*

Московское время Maskófskaye vrémya	*Moscow time*
время прибытия vrémya preebíyteeya	*time of arrival*
время отправления vrémya atpravlyéneeya	*time of departure*

What are these in Russian?

1. 60 minutes. ....

2. The time of day from sunrise to midday.

   ....

3. The time of day when it's dark.

   ....

4. The time of day when it's light. ....

5. Seven days are ....?

6. You want to know what time it is. What do you ask a Russian?

   ....

What time is it?

7. ....   8. ....   9. ....

10. ....   11. ....   12. ....

13. It is 9 o'clock and you want to go into a shop. You see the following sign on the door:

```
┌─────────────────────────────────┐
│  МАГАЗИН  ОТКРЫТ                 │
│  С 10³⁰    по    19 ч            │
└─────────────────────────────────┘
```

Can you start your shopping now? (Answer using **да** or **нет***)

....

14. At the station, the noticeboard shows the following time:

```
┌─────────────────────────────────┐
│ 09 │ МОСКОВСКОЕ  ВРЕМЯ           │
└─────────────────────────────────┘
```

What time is it in London?

....

(Look at this box!)

There are seven time zones in the Soviet Union. The European part uses Moscow time. When it's 12 o'clock in Moscow, it's 9 o'clock in England.

* (**открыт** = *open*)

БЕРЁЗКА
СУВЕНИРЫ · СССР

(a)
деньги dyéngee — *money*
рубль (р.) roobl — *rouble*
копейка (коп.) kapyéika — *kopeck*

одна копейка adná kapyéika	*1 kopeck*
две копейки dvye kapyéikee	*2 kopecks*
пять копеек pyat kapyéik	*5 kopecks*
десять копеек dyésit kapyéik	*10 kopecks*
один рубль adé§en roobl	*1 rouble*
три рубля tree rooblyá	*3 roubles*
пять рублей pyat rooblyéi	*5 roubles*
десять рублей dyésit rooblyéi	*10 roubles**

(b)
банк bank — *bank*
валюта valyóota — *currency*
пункт обмена валюты poonkt abmyéna valyóotiy — *currency exchange (office)*
курс koors — *exchange rate*
справка spráfka — *(currency exchange) certificate*

* See 8 (a) for the different forms.

9 Money and Shopping

(c)
магазин magazéen	*shop*
гастроном gastranóm	*food store*
продмаг pródmak	*food shop*
киоск keeósk	*kiosk*
универмаг ooneevirmák	*department store*
рынок ríynak	*market*

магазин "Берёзка" magazeen 'Biryózka'	*Beriozka shop* (special shop for foreigners where payment is in hard currency)
киоск "Сувениры" keeósk 'Soovinéeriy'	*souvenir kiosk*
Эту открытку, пожалуйста Étoo atkríytkoo, pazhálasta	*This postcard, please*
Эту книгу, пожалуйста Étoo knéegoo, pazhálasta	*This book, please*

(d)
цена tsiná	*price*
чек chek	*voucher, chit*
касса kássa	*cash desk*
квитанция kveetántseeya	*receipt*

Сколько это стоит? Skólka éta stóyit?	*How much is this?*
Я не понимаю Ya ni paneemáyoo	*I don't know*
Напишите мне это, пожалуйста Napeeshéetye mnye éta, pazhálasta	*Write me out a chit for this, please*

Read aloud the value of each of the following coins.

1. ....   2. ....   3. ....

4. ....   5. ....   6. ....

7. ....   8. ....

Look at this receipt.

9. In which shop were the purchases made?

....

10. How much money was spent?

....

9 Money and Shopping

- Russian money: 1 rouble is made up of 100 kopecks. There are coins for 1, 2, 3, 5, 10, 15, 20 and 50 kopecks and notes for 1, 3, 5, 10, 25, 50 and 100 roubles. One-rouble coins are issued to commemorate special occasions.

- Money can be changed at international airports, in banks and (Intourist) hotel exchange bureaux.

- Note however that roubles can only be changed back at the airport on departure. It is therefore advisable not to change too much money at first. Most purchases can in any case be made in hard currency in Beriozka shops.

- Buying something in a Russian shop generally involves the following procedure:
  - Find out the cost of the goods (most items on display have prices clearly marked).
  - Then pay this amount at a central cash desk, if necessary stating the name of the relevant department.
  - Take your receipt back to the counter and collect the goods.

- The following Russian shop signs can be seen everywhere:

АПТЕКА	Chemist's	ПАРИКМАХЕР-СКАЯ	Hairdresser's
БУЛОЧНАЯ ХЛЕБ	Baker's	РЕМОНТ	Repairs
ВИНО	Spirits	СОЮЗПЕЧАТЬ	Newsstand
ГАСТРОНОМ ПРОДУКТЫ	Foodstore	СУВЕНИРЫ	Souvenirs
МОЛОКО	Dairy, Milk	ТАБАК	Tobacconist
МЯСО	Butcher's	ЦВЕТЫ	Flowers
		ФРУКТЫ	Fruit
		РЫБА	Fishmonger's

(a)		
завтрак záftrak		breakfast
обед abyét		lunch
ужин óozhin		dinner, evening meal

(b)		
чашка cháshka		cup
стакан stakán		glass
бутылка bootíylka		bottle
тарелка taryélka		plate
чаша chásha		bowl
ложка lózhka		spoon
вилка véelka		fork
нож nozh		knife

(c)		
хлеб khlyep		bread
булочка bóolachka		roll
масло másla		butter
варенье varyéniye		jam
колбаса kalbasá		salami sausage
сосиски saséeskee		sausages (frankfurter type)

10 Meals

ветчина vitcheena	*ham*
яйцо yaitsó	*egg*
сыр siyr	*cheese*
блинчики bléenchikee	*pancakes*

кофе kófi	*coffee*
чай chai	*tea*
какао kaká'a	*cocoa*
кефир kiféer	*kefir (sour-milk drink)*

кофе с молоком kófi s malakóm	*coffee with milk*
чай без сахара chai byez sákhara	*tea without sugar*
стакан чая stakán chaya	*a glass of tea*

(*d*)

бутерброд booterbrót	*open sandwich*
ассорти мясное assartée misnóye	*assorted cold meat*
пирог peerók	*pie, pastry*
пирожное peerózhnaye	*pastry*

бутерброд с ветчиной booterbrót s vitcheenóy	*ham sandwich*
бутерброд с сыром booterbrót s síyram	*cheese sandwich*
бутерброд с колбасой booterbrót s kalbasóy	*salami sandwich*

What are the names of the meals in Russian?

1. The morning meal ....

2. The midday meal ....

3. The evening meal ....

Give the Russian for these items that you would find on the table.

4. ....

5. .... 6. .... 7. ....

8. .... 9. .... 10. ....

10 Meals

What is in these packets?

Give the answer in English.

11...

12...

13...

What would you expect to find in the glass below?

Give the answer in Russian.

14...

- Breakfast is very plentiful in the Soviet Union. There is likely to be assorted bread and rolls, butter, cheese, sausage and so on.

- Russian tea is often served in attractive glasses.

- Coffee does not always appeal to Western tastes. Moreover, it is very expensive.

- At street stands and snack-bars, tea and coffee are normally well sweetened. If you want your coffee or tea without sugar, you should say: "Без сахара" – byez sákhara.

11 Restaurants

(a) **ресторан** ristarán   *restaurant*
    кафе kafe   *cafe*
    закусочная zakóosachnaya   *snack-bar*   ⎫ basic,
    шашлычная shashlíychnaya   *kebab house* ⎬ self-
    столовая stalóvaya   *cafeteria*   ⎭ service
    буфет boofyét   *snack-bar*
    бар bar   *bar*
    стол stol   *table*
    стул stool   *chair*
    место myésta   *place*

(b) **меню** minyóo   *menu*
    закуски zakóoskee   *starters, hors d'oeuvres*
    первое pyérvaye   *first course* (usually soup)
    второе ftaróye   *main course* (= second course)
    десерт disyért   *dessert*

Дайте, пожалуйста, меню   *The menu, please*
Dáeetye, pazhálasta, minyóo

Я возьму ...   *I'll have ...*
Ya vazmóo ...

Что вы будете пить?   *What would you like to drink?*
Shto viy bóoditye peet?

(c) **сахар** sákhar   *sugar*
    соль sol   *salt*
    перец pyérits   *pepper*
    горчица garchéetsa   *mustard*
    уксус óoksoos   *vinegar*

(d) **официант** afeetsiánt   *waiter*
    девушка dyévooshka   *waitress*

Получите с нас, пожалуйста! *The bill, please!*
Paloochéetye, s␣nas, pazhalasta!

What are these in Russian?

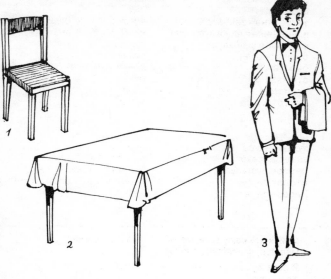

1. .... 2. .... 3. ....

4. What is the list of dishes called in Russian? ....

5. What do you eat before the main course?

....

6. What is the name of the sweet course in Russian?

....

7. What condiments do you take with your meat?

.... and ....

8. What do you sweeten your tea with? ....

11 Restaurants

- The Soviet Union does not have as many restaurants, bars, snack bars etc. as we are accustomed to at home.

- Many restaurants are attached to large hotels.

- Russian menus are often very extensive, but only the dishes marked with a price are on offer.

- There is also a series of private or so-called co-operative restaurants. The food here is generally more expensive than in state restaurants.

- Russian eating places normally shut at 11 pm.

(a) **Закуски** Zakóoskee   *Starters*
   Жульен из птицы   *Chicken au gratin*
   Zhoolyén eez ptéetsiy
   Грибы в сметане   *Mushrooms in sour cream*
   Greebíy f smitáni
   суп soop   *soup*
   щи shchee   *cabbage soup*
   борщ borshch   *beetroot soup, borsch*
   солянка salyánka   *spiced soup with smoked meat
                                        or fish*
   лапша lápsha   *noodle soup*

(b) **Мясо** Myása   *Meat*
   филе feeláy   *fillet steak*
   бифштекс bifshtéks   *beefsteak*
   печёнка pichónka   *liver*
   ветчина vitcheená   *ham*
   котлета katlyéta   *chop*
   шашлык shashlíyk   *shashlik, kebab*
   биточки beetóchkee   *meatballs*

12 Starters, Meat, Fish

Филе по-русски Feeláy pa-róoskee	*Fillet steak Russian-style*
Ветчина с гарниром Vitcheená s‿garnéeram	*Ham with vegetable garnish*
Биточки в сметане Beetóchkee f‿smitáni	*Meatballs in sour cream*
Бефстроганов Bifstróganaf	*Beef Stroganoff*
Салат мясной Salát misnóy	*Cold meat salad*

(c) **Птица** Ptéetsa — *Poultry*
курица kóoreetsa — *chicken*
яйца yaitsá — *eggs*
омлет amlyét — *omelette*
блины bleeníy — *buckwheat pancakes*

Омлет с ветчиной Amlyét s‿vitcheenóy	*Ham omelette*
Яйца под майонезом Yaitsá pad mayanézam	*Egg mayonnaise*

(d) **Рыба** Ríyba — *Fish*
севрюга sivryóoga — *sevruga (type of sturgeon)*
судак soodák — *pike-perch*
икра eekrá — *caviar*

осетрина asitréena	*sturgeon*
икра кетовая eekrá kyétavaya	*red caviar*

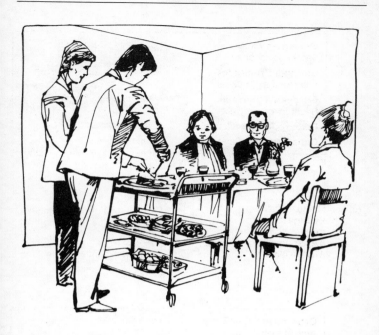

The waiter is taking orders.

1. You would like sturgeon for starters. What do you say?

   ....

2. Now ask for the famous Russian beetroot soup...

   ....

3. ... and the famous cabbage soup.

   ....

4. For the main course, order meatballs in sour cream.

   ....

12 Starters, Meat, Fish

What dishes are being served here?

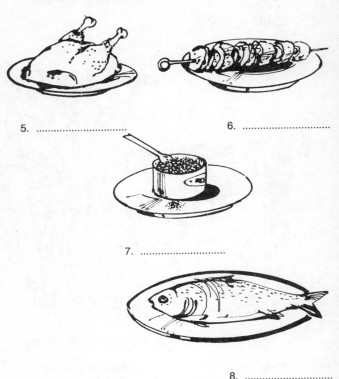

5. ....

6. ....

7. ....

8. ....

- There is usually a good choice of starters in Russian restaurants, e.g. fish, cold meats and salami, mushrooms, vegetable dishes.

- Russian cooking is particularly noted for its soups.

- The most famous Russian speciality is caviar (**икра**). Black caviar comes from the sturgeon, red caviar from salmon. Caviar can be bought in tins, and is very expensive in the Soviet Union as well as abroad.

(a)

Овощи Óvashchee		*Vegetables*
картофель kartófil		*potatoes*
капуста kapóosta		*cabbage*
кислая капуста kéeslaya kapóosta		*pickled cabbage*
огурец agooryéts		*cucumber*
фасоль fasól		*beans*
горох garókh		*peas*
помидоры pameedóriy		*tomatoes*
лук look		*onions*
морковь markóf		*carrots*
редис ridées		*radishes*
грибы greebíy		*mushrooms*
рис rees		*rice*

13 Vegetables, Fruit, Desserts

Салат из огурцов Salát eez agoortsóf	*Cucumber salad*
Салат из помидоров Salát eez pameedóraf	*Tomato salad*
Грибы в сметане Greebíy f smitáni	*Mushrooms in sour cream*

(b)

Фрукты Fróoktiy	*Fruit*
яблоко yáblaka	*apple*
апельсин apyelséen	*orange*
вишня véeshnya	*cherry*
черешня chiryéshnya	*sweet cherry*
персик pyérseek	*peach*
слива sléeva	*plum*
орех aryékh	*nuts*

(c)

Десерт Disyért	*Dessert*
компот kampót	*fruit compote*
мороженое marózhenaye	*ice cream*
вафли váflee	*waffles*
торт tort	*cake*
пирожное peerózhnaye	*pastry*
конфеты kanfyétiy	*sweets*
шоколад shakalát	*chocolate*

Пирог яблочный Peerók yáblachniy	*Apple pie*
Шоколадное мороженое Shakaládniye marózhenaye	*Chocolate ice-cream*

What are these in Russian?

1. .... 2. .... 3. ....

4. .... 5. .... 6. ....

7. .... 8. .... 9. ....

13 Vegetables, Fruit, Desserts

Here is the lunchtime menu for a Leningrad restaurant.

Can you name the dishes in the illustrations, and write them on the menu?

1.

2.

3.

4.

5.

6.

7.

Меню
ресторан

1. _____
2. _____
3. _____
4. _____
5. _____
6. _____
7. _____

- Ice-creams are particularly delicious in Russia, and are very popular not only in summer but also in cold weather.

(a) **минеральная вода**   *mineral water*
     minirálnaya vadá
     лимонад leemanát   *(type of) lemonade*
     сок sok   *juice*
     кофе kófi   *coffee*
     чай chai   *tea*
     молоко malakó   *milk*

14 Drinking and Smoking

фруктовый сок frooktóviy sok	*fruit juice*
кофе с молоком kófi s malakóm	*coffee with milk*
чай с лимоном chai s limónam	*tea with lemon*

(b)

пиво péeva	*beer*
квас kvas	*kvass* (weak alcoholic drink made from fermented bread, malt, honey, etc.)
водка vótka	*vodka*
коньяк kanyák	*cognac*
вино veenó	*wine*
шампанское shampánskaye	*champagne,* *sparkling white wine*

100 грамм водки, пожалуйста Sto gram vótkee, pazhálasta	*100 grams of vodka, please*
На здоровье! Na zdaróvye!	*Your health!*

(c)

сигарета seegaryéta	*cigarette*
папироса papeerósa	*Russian cigarette*
табак tabák	*tobacco*
зажигалка zazheegálka	*lighter*
спички spéechkee	*matches*

Не курить!
Ni kooréet!
У нас не курят }
Oo nas ni kóorya

No smoking!

Order the following non-alcoholic drinks:

1. A coffee. ....

2. A tea with lemon. ....

3. A mineral water. ....

4. A fruit juice. ....

Now order these alcoholic drinks:

5. A beer. ....

6. 100 grams of vodka. ....

7. Russian champagne. ....

8. You are drinking a toast with Russian friends. What do you say?

....

14 Drinking and Smoking

What are these in Russian?

9. .... 10. ....

11. .... 12. ....

- A typical Russian low-alcohol drink is *kvass* (**квас**), which looks like beer and is made from bread, honey, malt and other ingredients. In summer, you can buy it on the street from special lorries.

- One of the best-known brands of Russian beer is *Zhigulyóvskoye* (**Жигулёвское**).

- The most famous Russian drink is vodka (**водка**). There are many different types of vodka, e.g. *Psheníchnaya* (**Пшеничная**), made from wheat. Vodka along with other spirits is ordered by weight in grams: e.g. 50 grams of vodka, 100 grams of vodka.

- The Russians have two kinds of cigarette: cigarettes as we know them, and Russian-type cigarettes (*papeerósee*). These are 'half' cigarettes, smoked through long cardboard tubes. They are very cheap.

(a)
турист tooréest		*tourist*
гид geed		*guide*
переводчик pirivótcheek		*interpreter*
путеводитель pootivadéetyel		*guidebook*

(b)
осмотр asmótr		visit
музей moozyéi		museum
галерея galiryéya		gallery
замок zámak		castle
собор sabór		cathedral
икона eekóna		icon
монастырь manastíyr		monastery
мавзолей mavzalyéi		mausoleum
памятник pámitneek		monument
статуя státooya		statue

Кремль Kryeml	*Kremlin*
Мавзолей Ленина Mavzalyéi Lyéneena	*Lenin's tomb*
Крейсер "Аврора" Kréyser 'Avróra'	*Battleship 'Aurora'* (In Leningrad)

15 Sightseeing and Entertainment

(c)	**театр** tiátr	*theatre*
	опера ópira	*opera*
	балет balyét	*ballet*
	концерт kantsyért	*concert*
	цирк tseerk	*circus*
	кино keenó	*cinema*
	программа pragrámma	*programme*
	гардероб gardiróp	*cloakroom*
	партер partyér	*stalls*
	амфитеатр amfeetiátr	*amphitheatre, rear stalls*
	ярус yároos	*circle, tier*
	бельэтаж biletázh	*dress circle*
	ряд ryat	*row*
	место myésta	*seat*
	пластинка plastéenka	*record*
	народные песни	*folk songs*
	naródniye pyésnee	
	балалайка balaláika	*balalaika*

Болшой театр Balshóy tiátr	*Bolshoi Theatre*
ряд 10, место 5 ryat dyésit, myésta pyat	*row 10, seat no. 5*

(d)	**касса музея** kássa moozyéya	*museum ticket desk*
	входной билет fkhatnóy beelyét	*entrance ticket*
	вход fkhot	*entrance*
	выход víykhat	*exit*
	открыто atkríyta	*open*
	закрыто zakríyta	*closed*
	сувенир soovinéer	*souvenir*

Вход в музей Fkhot f‿moozyéi	*Entrance to museum*
Входа нет Fkhóda nyet	*No entrance*
Выход Víykhat	*Exit*

Do you recognise these tourist attractions? Can you name them?

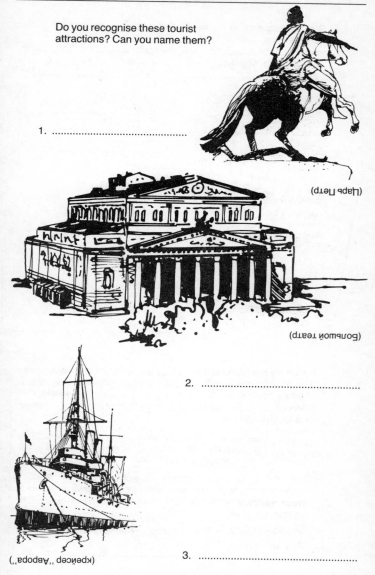

(Царь Петр)

1. ....

(Большой театр)

2. ....

(крейсер „Аврора")

3. ....

15 Sightseeing and Entertainment

Give the English equivalent of these notices which can be found in a museum.

ВХОД В МУЗЕЙ

КАССА МУЗЕЯ

4. .... 5. ....

ГАРДЕРОБ

СУВЕНИРЫ

6. .... 7. ....

ГОС. МУЗЕЙ
МОСКОВСКОГО КРЕМЛЯ

709945

МУЗЕЙ—СОБОР

ВХОДНОЙ БИЛЕТ

Сер. ББ-001

Цена 15 коп.

Мгт0 з.276—81

Look at this entrance ticket.

8. What tourist attraction is it for?

....

9. In what grounds can this be found?

....

- Lenin's tomb is open every day except Mondays from 10 am to 1 pm. Visitors wait in an orderly queue which can be up to a mile long. Large bags and cameras are not permitted, and visitors should be respectably dressed. Smoking is not allowed in Red Square.

- Soviet ballet, opera and concerts are world famous. The beautiful Bolshoi Theatre, built in 1776, has 5 tiers and seats 2150 people. It is sold out every day.

- Intourist can help in obtaining theatre tickets. Other methods of getting hold of tickets are: from kiosks showing the sign **театры**; last-minute returns in front of the theatre just before curtain-up.

- Gramophone records are readily available and comparatively cheap.

(a) **маршрут** marshróot   *route, itinerary*
     экскурсия ekskóorseeya   *excursion*

(b) **горы** góriy   *mountains*
     гора gará   *mountain, hill*
     долина daléena   *valley*
     лес lyes   *wood*
     степь styep   *steppe*
     тайга taigá   *taiga*
     река riká   *river*
     море mórye   *sea*
     озеро ózira   *lake*
     пляж plyazh   *beach*

16 Excursions and Recreation

Чёрное море Chórnoye mórye	Black Sea
озеро Байкал ózira Baikál	Lake Baikal
Волга Vólga	the Volga
Днепр Dnyepr	the Dnieper
Нева Nyéva	the Nieva
Кавказ Kafkáz	the Caucasus
Урал Oorál	the Urals
Крым Kriym	the Crimea
Украина Ookraéena	the Ukraine

(c)
спорт sport	sport
стадион stadeeón	stadium
кегельбан kegelbán	bowling-alley
бассейн bassyéin	swimming pool
шахматы shákhmatiy	chess
шахматист shakhmatéest	chess-player
охота akhóta	hunting
охотник akhótneek	huntsman

играть в шахматы eegrát f_shákhmatiy	to play chess
ходить на лыжах khadéet na líyzhakh	to go skiing
кататься на коньках katátsa na kankákh	to go skating

(d)
фотоаппарат fota-aparát	camera
фотография fotagráfeeya	photography
плёнка plyónka	film
диапозитивы deeapazitéeviy	slides
вспышка fspíyshka	flash

What can you see in these pictures? Answer in Russian.

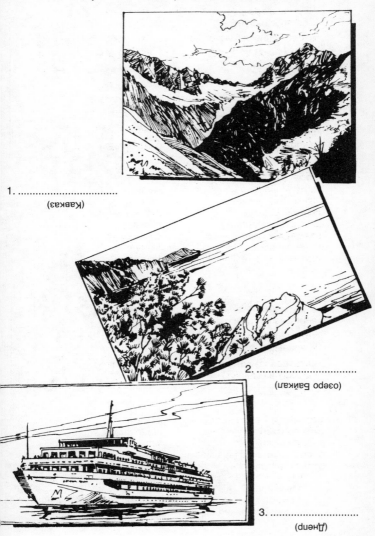

1. ....
(Кавказ)

2. ....
(озеро Байкал)

3. ....
(Днепр)

16 Excursions and Recreation

What are these in Russian?

4. ....

5. ....

6. ....

7. ....

What are these men?

8. ....

9. ....

- Intourist offers skiing trips to the Caucasus mountains for the active tourist. At the moment, the trips are to Gudari, but Intourist hope to expand their list of destinations. Holidays should be booked through individual tour operators.

(a)
погода pagóda	*weather*
температура timpiratóora	*temperature*
градус grádoos	*degree*

температура ночью и днём timpiratóora nóchoo ee dnyom	*the temperature by night* *and day*
около 0 градусов ókala noolá grádoosaf	*around 0 degrees*
1-5 градусов тепла adéen-pyat grádoosaf tiplá	*plus 1 to 5 degrees*

17 The Weather

(b) **хорошая погода**   *fine weather*
kharóshaya pagóda
солнце sóntse   *sun*
тепло tipló   *warmth*
жара zhará   *heat*
весна visná   *spring*
лето lyéta   *summer*

Солнце светит   *The sun is shining*
Sóntse svyéteet
тёплая погода   *warm weather*
tyóplaya pagóda
жарко zhárka   *it's hot*

(c) **плохая погода**   *bad weather*
plakháya pagóda
осадки asátkee   *precipitation*
дождь dozht   *rain*
облако óblaka   *cloud*
гроза grazá   *storm*
ветер vyétir   *wind*
буря bóorya   *gale*
туман toomán   *mist*
зонтик zónteek   *umbrella*
осень ósyen   *autumn*

Дождь идёт Dozht eedyót	*It's raining*

(d) **холод** khólat   *cold*
холодно khóladna   *it's cold*
снег snyek   *snow*
мороз maróz   *frost*
гололедица galalyédeetsa   *ice*
зима zeemá   *winter*

Снег идёт Snyek eedyót	*It's snowing*

What is the weather like?

1. .... 2. ....

Look at these television pictures.

ЛЕНИНГРАД
ОКОЛО +10

3. For which town is this forecast valid?

   ....

4. What is the predicted temperature?

   ....

+12
ЕРЕВАН

5. For which town is this forecast valid?

   ....

6. What is the temperature likely to be?

   ....

17 The Weather

Here are two weather forecasts from the newspaper **Правда**:

a)
ПОГОДА

7—8 января в Москве и Подмосковье ожидаются небольшие осадки, порывистый ветер, на дорогах гололедица, температура ночью и днем около 0 градусов.

b)
ПОГОДА

В ближайшие двое суток в Москве и Московской области пройдут кратковременные дожди, температура днем от 9 до 14 градусов тепла.

7. Compare the two forecasts. Which do you think refers to winter and which to spring?

Answer these questions using **да** or **нет**:

8. Is there any mention of rain or precipitation in either forecast?

....

9. Does forecast (*a*) refer to ice?

....

10. Does forecast (*b*) refer to wind?

....

- Average temperatures in Moscow (in degrees celsius) are as follows: January −10, February −8, March −4, April +4, May +13, June +16, July +19, August +16, September +10, October +4, November −2, December −7.
- During the thaw in the New Year, it is advisable to take footwear suitable for wading through mud and slush.

ТЕЛЕФОН

18 Post Office and Telephone

(a) **почта** póchta — *post*
почтамт pachtámt — *post office*
почтовый ящик — *post box*
pachtóviy yáshcheek

Где почтамт? — *Where is the post office?*
Gdye pachtámt?

(b) **письмо** peesmó — *letter*
конверт kanvyért — *envelope*
открытка atkríytka — *postcard*
телеграмма tiligrámma — *telegram*
марка márka — *stamp*
адрес ádris — *address*
куда koodá — *where to* ⎫ printed on postcards
кому kamóo — *to whom* ⎭ and envelopes

Сколько стоит открытка в Англию? — *How much is a postcard to England?*
Skólka stóyit atkríytka f,Ángleeyoo?

Пять марок за 50 копеек, пожалуйста — *Five stamps at 50 kopecks, please*
Pyat márak za pitdisyák kapyéek, pazhálasta

(c) **телефон** tilifón — *telephone*
номер телефона — *telephone number*
nómir tilifóna
телефонная будка — *telephone box*
tilifónaya bóotka
телефон-автомат — *pay phone*
tilifón-aftamát

Где телефон? Gdye tilifón? — *Where's the phone?*

What are these in Russian?

1. ....

2. ....

3. ....

4. ....

5. ....

18 Post Office and Telephone

6. You want to know how much a postcard to England costs. What do you ask the counter clerk?

   ....

7. You want five stamps at 50 kopecks. How do you ask for them?

   ....

8. What is this in Russian?

   ....

9. You want to know where the phone is. What do you ask?

   ....

- Post boxes are red or blue: red boxes are for local mail, blue ones for other destinations and abroad.
- There are no telephone directories in phone boxes.
- If you want to make a local call from a phone box, insert a 2-kopeck piece or two 1-kopeck pieces into the slot.

(a)

пальто paltó	coat
плащ plashch	raincoat
шапка shápka	cap
шарф sharf	scarf
перчатки pirchátkee	gloves
свитер svéetir	sweater
брюки bryóokee	trousers
блузка blóozka	blouse
юбка yóopka	skirt
платье plátye	dress

Этот шарф, пожалуйста État sharf, pazhálasta	*This scarf, please*
Эту меховую шапку, пожалуйста Étoo mikhavóoyoo shápkoo, pazhálasta	*This fur hat, please*

19 Clothing and Toiletries

(*b*) **ботинки** batéenkee — *shoes* (men's), *boots*
туфли tóoflee — *shoes* (women's)
носки naskée — *socks*
чулки chóolkee — *stockings*
колготки kalgótkee — *tights*

(*c*) **белый** byéliy — *white*
чёрный chórniy — *black*
серый syériy — *grey*
красный krásniy — *red*
зелёный zilyóniy — *green*
синий séenee — *blue* (dark)
голубой galoobóy — *blue* (light)
жёлтый zhóltiy — *yellow*
коричневый karéechniviy — *brown*

(*d*) **мыло** míyla — *soap*
полотенце palatyéntsi — *towel*
электробритва eliktrabréetva — *electric razor*
вата váta — *cotton wool*
очки achkée — *glasses*
парикмахерская pareekmákhirskaya — *hairdresser's*

What are these garments in Russian?

1............................   2..............................

What are these items in Russian?

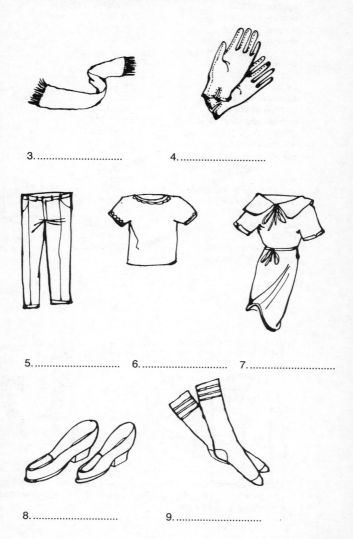

3. ....

4. ....

5. ....

6. ....

7. ....

8. ....

9. ....

10. You ask the assistant to show you a particular scarf. What do you say?

....

11. Now ask her to show you a particular fur hat.

....

What are these in Russian?

12. .... 13. .... 14. ....

15. What kind of headgear is this lady wearing?

....

– Many Russians wear attractive fur hats in winter. These hats can only be purchased from Beriozka shops, where they cost between £50 and £500.

(a) **авария** aváreeya — *accident*
пункт технического обслуживания — *repairs garage*
poonkt tikhnéechiskava apslóozheevaneeya
милиция miléetseeya — *police*
милиционер mileetsianyér — *policeman*

(b) **болеть** balýet — *to be ill*

У меня болит голова — *I've got a headache*
Oo minyá baléet galavá
У меня болит желудок — *I've got a stomach ache*
Oo minyá baléet zhilóodak
У меня жар — *I've got a temperature*
Oo minyá zhar

(c) **аптека** aptyéka — *chemist's*
пластырь plástiyr — *sticking plaster*
врач vrach — *doctor*
зубной врач zoopnóy vrach — *dentist*
больница balnéetsa — *hospital*

Где аптека? Gdye aptyéka? — *Where's the chemist's?*
Вызовите, пожалуйста, врача — *Call the doctor, please*
Viyzavéetye, pazhálasta, vrachá

(d) **Внимание!** Vneemáneeye! — *Look out!*
Осторожно! Astarózhna! — *Careful!*
На помощь! Na pómashch! — *Help!*
Запасной выход — *Emergency exit*
Zapasnóy víykhat

Answers

Practise the Russian Alphabet
Tourist, bank, bureau, cheque, cash desk, stop
Film, telephone, theatre, opera, ballet, concert, university
Professor, economist, student, institute, diploma, microscope, catalogue, lexicon, literature, journal,
Tolstoy, Anna Karenina, actress, radio.

1 General Expressions
1 Здравствуй, Пётр. 2 Как дела? 3 Хорошо. 4 До свидания. 5 Здравствуйте. 6 Ваш паспорт,
пожалуйста. 7 Вот мой паспорт. 8 Спасибо. 9 (a) Да. (b) Нет. 10 Простите. 11 Пожалуйста.

2 Arrival and Departure
1 Passport control. 2 Customs. 3 Чемодан. 4 Сумка. 5 Я англичанин (m.)/Я англичанка (f.). 6 Я из
Англии. 7 Ваша Фамилия? 8 Моя Фамилия – Jones. 9 Я не понимаю. 10 (a) СССР (Советский
Союз). (b) Великобритания. (c) Австралия.

3 Driving a Car
1 Автомобиль, машина. 2 Грузовик. 3 (Авто)стоянка. 4 Стоянка запрещена. 5 Пункт технического
обслуживания. 6 Заправочная станция.

4 Finding Your Way
1 (a) North. (b) East. (c) South. (d) West. 2 Прямо. 3 Направо. 4 Переход. 5 Направо. 6 Налево. 7 Да.

5 Public Transport
1 Platform 5. 2. Leningrad. 3 Exit to the town and taxis. 4 Колхозная (Kolkhoznaya). 5 Маяковская
(Mayakovskaya). 6 Следующая станция Смоленская (Next stop Smolenskaya). 7 Trolleybus. 8
Leningrad.

6 Accommodation
1 Постель. 2 Ключ. 3 Пожалуйста, ключ от номера сто двадцать. 4 No. 1. 5 16.08 and 19.26. 6
18.55. 7 19.14. 8 Ил. шестьдесят два. 9 Одиннадцать. 10 Четыре. 11 Семь. 12 Пятьдесят грамм
водки. 13 Сто грамм водки.

7 Numbers, Weights and Measures
1 (Номер) десять. 2 (Номер) сто двадцать. 3. Двести двенадцать. 4 (Номер) семьдесят пять. 5
16.08 and 19.26. 6 18.55. 7 19.14. 8 Ил. шестьдесят два. 9 Одиннадцать. 10 Четыре. 11 Семь. 12
Пятьдесят грамм водки. 13 Сто грамм водки.

8 Times and Dates
1 Час. 2 Утро. 3 Ночь. 4 День. 5 Неделя. 6 Который час? 7 Один час. 8 Два часа. 9 Шесть часов.
10 Восемь часов. 11 Девять часов. 12 Десять часов. 13 Нет. 14 Шесть часов.

9 Money and Shopping
1 Одна копейка. 2 Две копейки. 3 Три копейки. 4 Пять копеек. 5 Десять копеек. 6 Пятнадцать
копеек. 7 Двадцать копеек. 8 Пятьдесят. 9 Foodstore. 10 Три рубля четырнадцать копеек.

10 Meals
1 Завтрак. 2 Обед. 3 Ужин. 4 Чашка. 5 Стакан. 6 Вилка. 7 Тарелка. 8 Нож. 9 Ложка. 10 Бутылка.
11 Butter. 12 Cheese. 13 Kefir. 14 Стакан чая.

11 Restaurants
1 Стул. 2 Стол. 3 Официант. 4 Меню. 5 Закуски. 6 Десерт. 7 Соль, перец. 8 Сахар.

12 Starters, Meat, Fish
1 Осетрина, пожалуйста. 2 Борщ, пожалуйста. 3 Щи, пожалуйста. 4 Биточки в сметане,
пожалуйста. 5 Курица. 6 Шашлык. 7 Икра. 8 Рыба.

13 Vegetables, Fruit, Desserts
1 Фасоль. 2 Лук. 3 Огурец. 4 Морковь. 5 Помидоры. 6 Грибы. 7 Слива. 8 Яблоко. 9 Вишня. 10 (i)
Масло. (ii) Бифштекс. (iii) Суп. (iv) Рыба. (v) Кофе. (vi) Мороженое. (vii) Бутерброд.

14 Drinking and Smoking
1 Кофе, пожалуйста. 2 Чай с лимоном. 3 Минеральная вода. 4 Фруктовый сок, пожалуйста. 5
Пиво, пожалуйста. 6 Сто грамм водки. 7 Шампанское, пожалуйста. 8 На здоровье! 9 Сигарета. 10
Папироса. 11 Спички. 12 Зажигалка.

15 Sightseeing and Entertainment
1 Peter the Great (Tsar Peter). 2 The Bolshoi Theatre. 3 The battleship 'Aurora'. 4 Entrance to museum. 5
Museum ticket desk. 6 Cloakroom. 7 Souvenirs. 8 Cathedral museum. 9 The Kremlin.

16 Excursions and Recreation
1 Кавказ. 2 Озеро Байкал. 3 Днепр. 4 Фотоаппарат. 5 Вспышка. 6 Пленка. 7 Диапозитивы. 8
Шахматист. 9 Охотник.

17 The Weather
1 Дождь идёт. 2 Хорошая погода/Солнце светит. 3 Leningrad. 4 +10 degrees. 5 Yerevan. 6 +12
degrees. 7 (a) Winter. (b) Spring. 8. Да. – (a) precipitation, (b) rain. 9. Да. 10 Нет.

18 Post Office and Telephone
1 Открытка. 2 Конверт. 3 Марка. 4 Телеграмма. 5 Почтовый ящик. 6 Сколько стоит открытка в
Англию? 7 Пять марок за пятьдесят копеек, пожалуйста. 8 Телефон. 9 Где телефон?

19 Clothing and Toiletries
1 Пальто. 2 Шапка. 3 Шарф. 4 Перчатки. 5 Брюки. 6 Блузка. 7 Платье. 8 Туфли. 9 Носки. 10 Этот
шарф, пожалуйста. 11 Эту меховую шапку, пожалуйста. 12 Электробритва. 13 Полотенце. 14
Очки. 15 Меховую шапку.

Russian-English Vocabulary

авария accident 20a
Австралия Australia 2c
автобус bus 5d
автомагистраль motorway 3b
автомобиль car 3a
автостоянка car park 3c
администратор manager 6a
адрес address 2b, 18b
амфитеатр amphitheatre 15c
англичанка English woman 2c
англичанин Englishman 2c
английский English 2c
Англия England 2c
апельсин orange 13b
аптека chemist's 20c
ассорти мясное assorted cold meat 10d
аэропорт airport 5b
АЭРОФЛОТ AEROFLOT 5b

багаж luggage 2a
балалайка balalaika 15c
балет ballet 15c
банк bank 9b
бар bar 11a
бассейн swimming pool 16c
белый white 19c
бельэтаж dress circle 15c
бензин petrol 3c
билет ticket 5e
биточки meatballs 12b
бифштекс beefsteak 12b
блины pancakes 12c
блинчики pancakes 10c
блузка blouse 19a
болеть to be ill 20b
больница hospital 20c
борщ borsch, beetroot soup 12a
ботинки shoes, boots 19b
брюки trousers 19a
булочка bread roll 10c
булочная baker's 9
бульвар boulevard 4c
буря gale 17c
бутерброд sandwich 10d
бутылка bottle 10b
буфет snackbar 11a

вагон-ресторан dining-car 5a
валюта foreign currency 9b
ванна bath 6b
ванная bathroom 6b
варенье jam 10c
вата cotton wool 19d
вафли waffles 13c
ваш your 1f
Великобритания Great Britain 2c
весна spring 17b
ветер wind 17c
ветчина ham 10c, 12b

вечер evening 8b
виза visa 2b
вилка fork 10b
вино wine 9, 14b
вишня cherry 13b
внимание! look out! 20d
вода water 6b
вокзал station 5a
воскресенье Sunday 8c
восток East 4d
вот here is 1e
врач doctor 20c
время time 8c
время отправления departure time 8c
время прибытия arrival time 8c
вспышка flash 16d
вторник Tuesday 8c
второе main (second) course 11b
вы you 1f
вход entrance 5e, 15d
входной билет entrance ticket 15d
вчера yesterday 8b
вылет (departure) flight 5b
выход exit 5e, 15d

галерея gallery 15b
гардероб cloakroom 15c
гастроном food store 9c
где where 4d
гид guide 15a
год year 8c
гололедица ice 17d
голубой blue (light) 19c
гора hill, mountain 16b
город town 4b
горох peas 13a
горчица mustard 11c
горы mountains 16b
господин Mr 1d
госпожа Mrs 1d
гостиница hotel 6a
гость guest 6a
градус degree 17a
гражданство nationality 2c
грамм gram 7b
грибы mushrooms 13a
грузовик lorry 3a

да yes 1a
дата рождения date of birth 2b
двухместный номер double room 6b
девушка waitress, girl 11d
дежурная по этажу corridor attendant 6b
день day 8b
деньги money 9a
десерт dessert 11b, 13c
диапозитивы slides 16d
доброе утро good morning 1b
дождь rain 17c

Russian-English Vocabulary

долина valley 16b
дорога road 3b
дорожная карта road map 4a
до свидания goodbye 1b
душ shower 6b

жара heat 17b
жёлтый yellow 19c

завтра tomorrow 8b
завтрак breakfast 10a
зажигалка lighter 14c
закрыто closed 15d
закуска starter 11b, 12a
закусочная snackbar 11a
замок castle 15b
занято engaged 6d
запад West 4d
запасной выход emergency exit 5e, 20d
заправочная станция service station 3c
здравствуйте hello 1b
зелёный green 19c
зима winter 17d
зонтик umbrella 17c
зубной врач dentist 20c

икона ikon 15b
икра caviar 12d
имя first name 2b
ИНТУРИСТ INTOURIST 6a
информация information 5e

какао cocoa 10c
Канада Canada 2c
капуста cabbage 13a
карта map 4a
карта города town plan 4a
картофель potato 13a
касса cash desk 5e, 9d
касса музея museum ticket desk 15d
кафе cafe 11a
каюта cabin 5c
квас kvass 14b
квитанция receipt 6c, 9d
кегельбан bowling-alley 16c
кемпинг campsite 6a
кефир kefir 10c
кило kilo 7b
кино cinema 15c
киоск kiosk 9c
кислая капуста pickled cabbage 13a
ключ key 6b
когда when 8a
колбаса salami 10c
колготки tights 19b
комната room 6b
компот compote 13c
кому to whom 18b
конверт envelope 18b

конечно of course 1a
консульство consulate 2c
конфеты sweets 13c
концерт concert 15c
коньки skates 16c
коньяк cognac 14b
копейка kopeck 9a
коричневый brown 19c
котлета chop, cutlet 12b
кофе coffee 10c, 14a
красный red 19c
куда where to 18b
курица chicken 12c
курс exchange rate 9b

лапша noodle soup 12a
лес wood 16b
лето summer 17b
лимонад lemonade 14a
лифт lift 6b
ложка spoon 10b
лук onion 13a
лыжи skis 16c

мавзолей tomb 15b
магазин shop 9c
марка stamp 18b
маршрут route 16a
масло butter 10c, oil 3c
машина car 3a
меню menu 11b
место seat, place 11a, 15c
месяц month 8c
метро underground 5d
милиционер policeman 20a
милиция police 20a
минеральная вода mineral water 14a
минута minute 8a
много a lot 7b
мой my 1f
молоко milk 9, 14a
монастырь monastery 15b
море sea 16b
морковь carrot 13a
мороженое ice cream 13c
мороз frost 17d
мост bridge 4c
музей museum 15b
мыло soap 19d
мясо meat 9, 12b

налево left 4d
на помощь! help! 20d
направо right 4d
народные песни folk songs 15c
неделя week 8c
немного a little 7b
нет no 1a
ничего don't mention it 1c

Russian-English Vocabulary

Новая Зеландия New Zealand 2c
нож knife 10b
номер hotel room, number 6b
номер телефона telephone number 18c
носки socks 19b
ночь night 8b

обед lunch 10a
облако cloud 17c
овощи vegetables 13a
огурец cucumber 13a
одноместный номер single room 6b
озеро lake 16b
окно window, counter 5e
омлет omelette 12c
опера opera 15c
орех nut 13b
осадки precipitation 17c
осень autumn 17c
осетрина sturgeon 20d
осмотр visit 15b
остановка (bus) stop 5d
осторожно! careful! 20d
открытка postcard 18b
открыто open 15d
очки glasses 19d
официант waiter 11d
охота hunting 16c
охотник huntsman 16c

пальто coat 19a
памятник monument 15b
папироса Russian cigarette 14c
парикмахерская hairdresser's 19d
пароход steamer 5c
партер stalls 15c
паспорт passport 2b
пассажир passenger 5e
переводчик interpreter 15a
переулок alley 4c
переход underpass 4c, connections 5d
перец pepper 11c
персик peach 13b
перчатки gloves 19a
печёнка liver 12b
пиво beer 14b
пирог pie, pasty 10d
пирожное pastry 10c, 13c
письмо letter 18b
пить to drink 11b
пластинка record 15c
пластырь sticking plaster 20c
платье dress 19a
плащ raincoat 19a
плёнка film 16d
площадь square 4c
пляж beach 16b
погода weather 17a, 17b, 17c
подпись signature 2b

поезд train 5a
поездка journey 2a
пожалуйста please 1c
пол sex 2b
полдень midday 8b
полкило half a kilo 7b
полотенце towel 19d
помидоры tomatoes 13a
понедельник Monday 8c
посольство embassy 2c
постель bed 6b
почта post 18a
почтамт post office 18a
почтовый ящик post box 18a
права (driving) licence 3a
программа programme 15c
продмаг foodstore 9c
продукты foodstore 9
проспект avenue, prospect 3b, 4c
простите excuse me 1c
прямо straight on 4d
птица poultry 12c
пункт обмена валюты currency exchange
  bureau 9b
пункт технического обслуживания
  repairs garage 3c, 20a
путеводитель guidebook 15a
путь track, platform 5a
пятница Friday 8c

ракета hydrofoil 5c
расписание timetable 5e
редис radish 13a
река river 16b
ресторан restaurant 11a
рис rice 13a
рубль rouble 9a
рыба fish 12d
рынок market 9c
ряд row 15c

самолёт aeroplane 5b
сахар sugar 11c
свитер sweater 19a
свободно free 6d
север North 4d
севрюга sevruga (sturgeon) 12d
сегодня today 8b
серый grey 19c
сигарета cigarette 14c
синий blue (dark) 19c
сколько how much, how many 7b
слива plum 13b
собор cathedral 15b
сок juice 14a
солнце sun 17b
солянка spiced soup 12a
соль salt 11c
сосиски sausages 10c

Russian-English Vocabulary

снег snow 17d
спальный вагон sleeping car 5a
спасибо thank you 1c
спички matches 14c
спорт sport 16c
справка certificate 9b
справки enquiries 5e
среда Wednesday 8c
СССР USSR 2c
стадион stadium 16c
стакан glass 10b, 10c
станция (underground) station 5d
статуя statue 15b
степь steppe 16b
стоимость номера price of the room 6c
стол table 11a
столица capital 4b
столовая cafeteria 11a
стоп! stop! 3d
стоянка такси taxi rank 5d
стул chair 11a
суббота Saturday 8c
сувенир souvenir 15d
судак pike-perch 12d
сумка handbag 2a
суп soup 12a
сыр cheese 10c

табак tobacco 14c
тайга taiga 16b
такси taxi 5d
там there 4d
таможня customs 2a
тарелка plate 10b
театр theatre 15c
телеграмма telegram 18b
телефон telephone 18c
телефон-автомат pay phone 18c
телефонная будка telephone box 18c
температура temperature 17a
тепло warmth 17b
товарищ comrade 1d
торт cake 13c
трамвай tram 5d
троллейбус trolleybus 5d
туалеты toilets 6d
туман mist 17c
турист tourist 15a
тут here 4d
туфли shoes 19b

ужин dinner 10a
уксус vinegar 11c
улица street 4c
универмаг department store 9c
утро morning 8b
Уэльс Wales 2c

фамилия surname 2b

фасоль beans 13a
филе fillet 12b
фотоаппарат camera 16d
фотография photography 16d
фрукты fruit 13b

хлеб bread 10c
холод cold 17d
холодно it's cold 17d
хорошо good 1a

цена price 9d
центр города town centre 4b
цирк circus 15c

чай tea 10c, 14a
час hour 8a
часы watch, clock 8a
чаша bowl 10b
чашка cup 10b
чек voucher 9b
чемодан suitcase 2a
черешня sweet cherry 13b
чёрный black 19c
четверг Thursday 8c
чулки stockings 19b

шампанское champagne 14b
шапка cap 19a
шарф scarf 19a
шахматист chess-player 16c
шахматы chess 16c
шашлык shashlik 12b
шашлычная kebab house 11a
шина tyre 3a
шоколад chocolate 13c
шоссе main road 3b
Шотландия Scotland 2c

щи cabbage soup 12a

экскурсия excursion 16a
електробритва electric razor 19d
этаж floor, storey 6b
эта this (f.) 1e
это this is, this (n.) 1e
этот this (m.) 1e

юбка skirt 19a
юг South 4d

я I 1f
яблоко apple 13b
яйцо egg 10c
яйца eggs 12c
ярус circle, tier 15c

English-Russian Vocabulary

accident авария 20a
address адрес 2b, 18b
AEROFLOT АЭРОФЛОТ 5b
aeroplane самолёт 5b
airport аэропорт 5b
alley переулок 4c
a lot много 7b
amphitheatre амфитеатр 15c
apple яблоко 13b
arrival time время прибытия 8c
assorted cold meat ассорти мясное 10d
Australia Австралия 2c
autumn осень 17c
avenue проспект 3b, 4c

baker's булочная 9
balalaika балалайка 15c
ballet балет 15c
bank банк 9b
bar бар 11a
bath ванна 6b
bathroom ванная 6b
beach пляж 16b
beans фасоль 13a
bed постель 6b
beefsteak бифштекс 12b
beer пиво 14b
beetroot soup борщ 12a
black чёрный 19c
blouse блузка 19a
blue (dark) синий 19c
blue (light) голубой 19c
boots ботинки 19b
borsch борщ 12a
bottle бутылка 10b
boulevard бульвар 4c
bowl чаша 10b
bowling alley кегельбан 16c
bread хлеб 10c
bread roll булочка 10c
breakfast завтрак 10a
bridge мост 4c
brown коричневый 19c
bus автобус 5d
bus stop остановка 5d
butter масло 10c

cabbage капуста 13a
cabbage, pickled кислая капуста 13a
cabbage soup щи 12a
cabin каюта 5c
cafe кафе 11a
cafeteria столовая 11a
cake торт 10c
camera фотоаппарат 16d
campsite кемпинг 6a
Canada Канада 2a
cap шапка 19a
capital столица 4b

car автомобиль, машина 3a
careful! осторожно! 20d
car park автостоянка 3c
carrot морковь 13a
cash desk касса 5e, 9d
castle замок 15b
cathedral собор 15b
caviar икра 12d
certificate справка 9b
chair стул 11a
champagne шампанское 14b
cheese сыр 10c
chemist's аптека 20c
cherry вишня 13b
cherry, sweet черешня 13b
chess шахматы 16c
chess-player шахматист 16c
chicken курица 12c
chocolate шоколад 13c
chop котлета 12b
cigarette сигарета 14c
cigarette (Russian) папироса 14c
cinema кино 15c
circle (theat.) ярус 15c
circus цирк 15c
cloakroom гардероб 15c
clock часы 8a
closed закрыто 15d
cloud облако 17c
coat пальто 19a
cocoa какао 10c
coffee кофе 10c, 14a
cognac коньяк 14b
cold холод 17d
cold, it's – холодно 17d
compote компот 13c
comrade товарищ 1d
concert концерт 15c
connections переход 5d
consulate консульство 2c
corridor attendant дежурная по этажу 6b
cotton wool вата 19d
cucumber огурец 13a
cup чашка 10b
currency (foreign) валюта 9b
currency exchange bureau пункт обмена
   валюты 9b
customs таможня 2a

date of birth дата рождения 2b
day день 8b
degree градус 17a
dentist зубной врач 20c
department store универмаг 9c
departure time время отправления 8c
dessert десерт 11b, 13c
dining-car вагон-ресторан 5a
dinner ужин 10a
doctor врач 20c

English-Russian Vocabulary

don't mention it ничего 1c
double room двухместный номер 6b
dress платье 19a
dress circle бельэтаж 15c
to drink пить 11b

East восток 4d
egg яйцо 10c
eggs яйца 12c
electric razor электробритва 19d
embassy посольство 2c
emergency exit запасной выход 5e, 20d
engaged занято 6d
England Англия 2c
English английский 2c
Englishman англичанин 2c
English woman англичанка 2c
enquiries справки 5e
entrance вход 5e, 15d
entrance ticket входной билет 15d
envelope конверт 18b
evening вечер 8b
exchange rate курс 9b
excursion экскурсия 16a
excuse me простите 1c
exit выход 5e, 15d

fillet (steak) филе 12b
film плёнка 16d
first name имя 2b
fish рыба 12d
flash вспышка 16d
flight (departure) вылет 5b
floor (storey) этаж 6b
folk songs народные песни 15c
food store гастроном, продмаг 9c, продукты 9
foreign currency валюта 9b
fork вилка 10b
free свободно 6d
Friday пятница 8c
frost мороз 17d
fruit фрукты 13b

gale буря 17c
gallery галерея 15b
girl девушка 11d
glass стакан 10b, 10c
glasses очки 19d
gloves перчатки 19a
good хорошо 1a
goodbye до свидания 1b
good morning доброе утро 1b
gram грамм 7b
Great Britain Великобритания 2c
green зелёный 19c
grey серый 19c
guest гость 6a
guide гид 15a

guidebook путеводитель 15a

hairdresser's парикмахерская 19d
half a kilo полкило 7b
ham ветчина 10c, 12b
handbag сумка 2a
heat жара 17b
hello здравствуйте 1b
help! на помощь! 20d
here тут 4d
here is вот 1e
hill гора 16b
hospital больница 20c
hotel гостиница 6a
hotel room номер 6b
hour час 8a
how much, how many сколько 7b
hunting охота 16c
huntsman охотник 16c
hydrofoil ракета 5c

I я 1f
ice гололедица 17d
ice-cream мороженое 13c
icon икона 15b
ill, to be болеть 20b
information информация 5e
interpreter переводчик 15a
INTOURIST ИНТУРИСТ 6a

jam варенье 10c

kebab-house шашлычная 11a
kefir кефир 10c
key ключ 6b
kilo кило 7b
kiosk киоск 9c
knife нож 10b
kopeck копейка 9a
kvass квас 14b

lake озеро 16b
left налево 4d
lemonade лимонад 14a
letter письмо 18b
licence, driving права 3a
lift лифт 6b
lighter зажигалка 14c
little, a немного 7b
liver печёнка 12b
look out! внимание! 20d
lorry грузовик 3a
luggage багаж 2b
lunch обед 10a

main course второе 11b
manager администратор 6a
map карта 4a
market рынок 9c

English-Russian Vocabulary

matches спички 14c
meat мясо 9, 12b
meatballs биточки 12b
menu меню 11b
midday полдень 8b
milk молоко 9, 14a
mineral water минеральная вода 14a
minute минута 8a
mist туман 17c
monastery монастырь 15b
Monday понедельник 8c
money деньги 9a
month месяц 8c
monument памятник 15b
morning утро 8b
motorway автомагистраль 3b
mountains горы 16b
Mr господин 1d
Mrs госпожа 1d
museum музей 15b
museum ticket desk касса музея 15d
mushrooms грибы 13a
mustard горчица 11c
my мой (m.), моя (f.), моё (n.)

name (first) имя 2b
nationality гражданство 2c
New Zealand Новая Зеландия 2c
night ночь 8b
no нет 1a
noodle soup лапша 12a
North север 4d
number номер 6b

of course конечно 1a
oil масло 3c
omelette омлет 12c
onion лук 13a
open открыто 15d
opera опера 15c
orange апельсин 13b
pancakes блины 12c, блинчики 10c
passenger пассажир 5e
passport паспорт 2b
pastry пирожное 10c, 13c
pasty пирог 10d
peach персик 13b
peas горох 13a
pepper перец 11c
petrol бензин 3c
photography фотография 16d
pie пирог 10d
pike-perch судак 12d
please пожалуйста 1c
police милиция 20a
policeman милиционер 20a
place место 11a, 15c
plate тарелка 10b
platform путь 5a

plum слива 13b
post почта 18a
post box почтовый ящик 18a
postcard открытка 18b
post office почтамт 18a
potato картофель 13a
poultry птица 12b
precipitation осадки 17c
price цена 9d
price (of room) стоимость (номера) 6c
programme программа 15c

radish редис 13a
rain дождь 17c
raincoat плащ 19a
receipt квитанция 6c, 9d
record пластинка 15c
red красный 19c
repairs garage пункт технического
обслуживания 3c, 20a
restaurant ресторан 11a
rice рис 13a
right направо 4d
river река 16b
road дорога 3b
road, main шоссе 3b
road map дорожная карта 4a
room комната 6b
room (hotel) номер 6b
rouble рубль 9a
route маршрут 16a
row ряд 15c

salami колбаса 10c
salt соль 11c
sandwich бутерброд 10d
Saturday суббота 8c
sausages сосиски 10c
scarf шарф 19a
Scotland Шотландия 2c
sea море 16b
seat место 11a, 15c
service station заправочная станция 3c
sevruga севрюга 12d
sex пол 2b
shashlik шашлык 12b
shoes ботинки (men's), туфли (women's) 19b
shop магазин 9c
shower душ 6b
signature подпись 2b
single room одноместный номер 6b
skates коньки 16c
skirt юбка 19a
skis лыжи 16c
sleeping car спальный вагон 5a
slides диапозитивы 16d
snackbar буфет 11a, закусочная 11a
snow снег 17d
soap мыло 19d

English-Russian Vocabulary

socks носки 19b
soup суп 12a
South юг 4d
souvenir сувенир 15d
spoon ложка 10b
sport спорт 16c
spring весна 17b
square площадь 4c
stadium стадион 16c
stalls партер 15c
stamp марка 18b
starter закуска 11b, 12a
station вокзал 5a
station (underground) станция 5d
statue статуя 15b
steamer пароход 5c
steppe степь 16b
sticking plaster пластырь 20c
stockings чулки 19b
stop! стоп! 3d
stop (bus) остановка 5d
storey этаж 6b
storm гроза 17c
straight on прямо 4d
street улица 4c
sturgeon осетрина 20d
sugar сахар 11c
suitcase чемодан 2a
summer лето 17b
sun солнце 17b
Sunday воскресенье 8c
surname фамилия 2b
sweater свитер 19a
sweets конфеты 13c
swimming pool бассейн 16c

table стол 11a
taiga тайга 16b
taxi такси 5d
taxi rank стоянка такси 5d
tea чай 10c, 14a
telegram телеграмма 18b
telephone телефон 18c
telephone box телефонная будка 18c
telephone number номер телефона 18c
temperature температура 17a
thank you пожалуйста 1c
theatre театр 15c
there там 4d
this этот (m.), эта (f.), это (n.) 1e
this is . . . это . . . 1e
Thursday четверг 8c
ticket билет 5e
tier ярус 15c
tights колготки 15c
time время 8c
timetable расписание 5e
tobacco табак 14c
today сегодня 8b

toilets туалеты 6d
tomatoes помидоры 13a
tomb мавзолей 15b
tomorrow завтра 8b
tourist турист 15a
towel полотенце 19d
town город 4b
town centre центр города 4b
town plan карта города 4a
track путь 5a
train поезд 5a
tram трамвай 5d
trolleybus троллейбус 5d
trousers брюки 19a
Tuesday вторник 8c
tyre шина 3a

umbrella зонтик 17c
underground (tube) метро 5d
underpass переход 4c
USSR СССР 2c

valley долина 16b
vegetables овощи 13a
vinegar уксус 11c
visa виза 2b
visit осмотр 15b
voucher чек 9d

waffles вафли 13c
waiter официант 11d
waitress девушка 11d
Wales Уэльс 2c
warmth тепло 17b
watch часы 8a
water вода 6b
weather погода 17a, 17b, 17c
Wednesday среда 8c
week неделя 8c
West запад 4d
when когда 8a
where где 4d
where to куда 18b
white белый 19c
wind ветер 17c
window окно 5c
wine вино 9, 14b
winter зима 17d
wood лес 16b

year год 8c
yellow жёлтый 19c
yes да 1a
yesterday вчера 8b
you вы 1f
your ваш (m.), ваша (f.), ваше (n.) 1f